stonedesigns
for the home

stonedesigns
for the home

John T. Morris with Candace Walsh
Photographs by Robert Reck

Gibbs Smith, Publisher
TO ENRICH AND INSPIRE HUMANKIND
Salt Lake City | Charleston | Santa Fe | Santa Barbara

First Edition
08 09 10 11 12   5 4 3 2 1

Text © 2008 John T. Morris
Photographs © 2008 Robert Reck

Published by
Gibbs Smith, Publisher
P.O. Box 667
Layton, Utah 84041

Orders: 1.800.835.4993
www.gibbs-smith.com

Designed by Debra McQuiston
Printed and bound in China

Library of Congress Cataloging-in-Publication Data
Morris, John T.
Stone designs for the home / John T. Morris ; with
Candace Walsh ; photographs by Robert Reck. — 1st ed.
p. cm.
ISBN-13: 978-1-4236-0194-4
ISBN-10: 1-4236-0194-7
1. Building fittings—Design and construction. 2.
Stonemasonry. 3. Stone carving. I. Walsh, Candace.
II. Reck, Robert, 1945- III. Title.

TH6010.M67 2008
693'.1—dc22
2007042888

This book is dedicated to the following people: my mother and father, Edward and Julia Morris, and my wife, Barbara—the rocks upon which I stand; my children, Anna and Noah; and Robert Taylor, my teacher.

ACKNOWLEDGMENTS

A special thanks to all the workers who have helped me through the years. And thanks to Candace Walsh and Robert Reck, whose talent and inspiration helped me to complete this project.

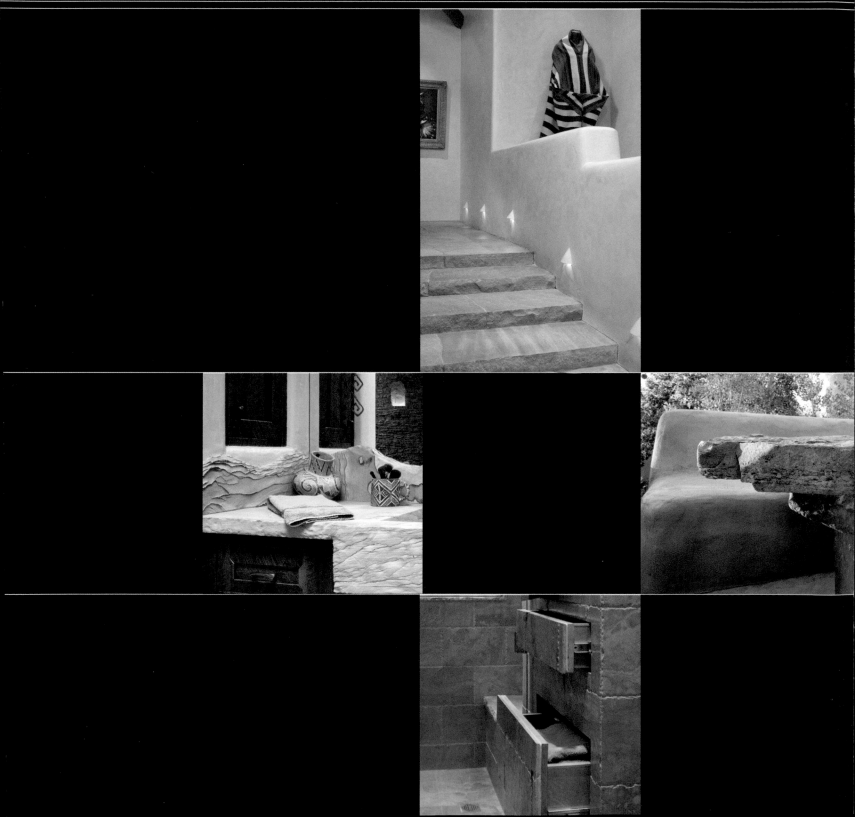

INTRODUCTION

Staggered flagstone steps and river rock retaining walls create a dynamic entrance to this home's front door.

I have always loved nature. I love the ocean, the grass, the sky, the clouds . . . so it's not surprising that I would fall in love with stone, the foundation of this beautiful earth. Stones are like clouds of the earth—they're never the same. Each one has its own individual shape, makeup, and coloration. Each stone's history shows in the way it's been eroded, exposed to the sun, and polished by water or other forces of nature. When building with stone, it comes down to me and my mind, where I want to place the stone, how I want to place it. It's open, like music. Each time I pick up a rock, there's a new song to be sung.

What I love about a stone project is the uninterrupted flow of a job unfolding toward completion. When I complete a project, no matter how small it is, the biggest reward I get—the biggest thrill—is not a paycheck or a pat on the back. It's standing back and looking at it and admiring my own work. I don't say this with arrogance; it's just that after all these years, I know so keenly when stonework is good, and I'm so exacting, that when I am able to feel like I am finished, that in itself is a reward. I don't sign my work. Just knowing that it's finished to my satisfaction is enough for me.

My journey in stone began with a single wish: to get away from New York City. I was filled with a young man's wanderlust, and I wanted to explore the world. While visiting my brother in New Mexico, I discovered a different world, with different plants, a different sky, and rocks I'd never seen before. It was like I was on another planet. I moved to New Mexico.

I had grown up in New Jersey, where everything is perfectly manicured. Even though I was surrounded by amazing stone projects—St. John the Divine Cathedral, St. Patrick's Cathedral, Trinity Church—I was blind to them; I took them for granted. It wasn't until I was living out west that I discovered the beauty of stone and my calling to work with it.

All my life I had wanted to be a rock-and-roll star, but when my two children came along, reality stepped in and I wondered how I would support them. I became a hustler for work. I delivered the newspaper, brought people's garbage to the dump, cleaned up properties, cut firewood for fifty dollars a cord. Friday, Saturday, and Sunday nights I worked at a truck stop, pumping gas and fixing tires.

Delivering newspapers one day in Santa Fe, I stopped to watch a man build a stone wall. He worked for landscape designer Jacques Cartier (also an acclaimed dancer

In the years

since I discovered stone, I've felt close to heaven.

and choreographer responsible for the creation of Santa Fe's Zozobra Fire Dancer). The process fascinated me. It was a wall with no mortar showing, yet it was made out of river rock. I wondered, "How does he make them all stay together? How is that done?" In New York, I had never seen work like that. It was the beginning of my first inkling that in doing such precise stonework, you can't let yourself be directed or led by time. It can't enter into the equation. Normally we think of jobs in terms of how much has to be done in increments of time. I saw him concentrating on doing the best job that he could. That's where his mind was. He wasn't thinking, "When will it be five o'clock?" As I watched him, I understood what was involved in building a wall from stone. "I can do this," I thought. I also noticed the stones that he was using were stones I had access to and could sell.

I brought him rocks. I saw what shapes and kinds of rock he wanted and I got them from the river, filling a gunnysack and drag-

ging it to my truck. My son, Noah, came with me. We also went up into the mountains, collecting rocks and firewood together and selling stone to Cuyamungue Stone Company. Eventually Robert Taylor, the owner of Cuyamungue Stone Company, asked me to come work for him full time. I lasted for twelve years, apprenticing the art of masonry: collecting, laying, cutting rock. I did it his way, and over time, I also developed my own methods.

Robert Taylor taught me the stonemasonry trade, and when I went out on my own, he sent jobs my way. I founded my company in 1985 and named it Stone Age 2000. After the year 2000 rolled around, we changed the name to New Mexico Stone. On my own, I had to bluff my way through so many projects. "Sure, I can do that," I'd say, and then wonder how I was going to do it. The most difficult part was learning to read blueprints and plans. I'd bring them home to my wife, Barbara, and she'd translate the plans for

The look of these walls was inspired by the work a stonemason did on the property thirty years ago. Coincidentally, I supplied that stonemason with the stones he used on the property.

me until I understood them on my own. Her expertise was invaluable. As a landscape designer, she knew all about blueprints and helped me to make the jobs happen until I became a prominent figure in the Santa Fe stone world.

Thirty years ago, scrabbling for my livelihood and cut off from dreams of being a successful musician, I felt so close to hell—going to work every day without a goal, without a glimpse of heaven to inspire me; trying to build a house without any money.

In the years since I discovered stone, I've felt close to heaven. My journey of mastering stone has also been a journey for the southwestern stone movement. My stonework is an example of stonework of the Southwest. Thirty years ago, all of the fancy stonework that you see in Tesuque and Las Campanas wasn't happening. The projects that I've completed with my team have led to this current level of appreciation and demand for quality stonework. We've raised awareness of the art in the region and in the world.

My work has been featured in *Architectural Digest* and other magazines, and I've been disappointed to note that the work my team and I have created is not given the proper description and credit. One recent photo in a national magazine was described as a "wall of uncut stone." Every single stone in that wall was cut, battered, beaten, and mauled into shapes that we insisted on. I don't think the lack of credit is intentional, just a lack of understanding. Bad stonework sticks out, but stonework done well can seem inevitable—so natural and timeless that you fail to see it on its own, if you don't yet have an eye for it. It blends in like the sky, the trees, and the land.

People look at me and think that my goal was always to be where I am today. Not true. It was a mixture of chance, instinct, timing, and years of hard work. And yet it still feels like fate.

Ground cover growing between the flagstone pavers adds to the soft, natural look of this landscape.

Smooth, round river rocks used in these walls create a gentle look that works well with the rounded edges of the home's pueblo-style architecture.

FACING: This stone archway was so fulfilling for me to build because it started out as a challenge—an itch I had to make a beautiful archway—and it ended up fitting together perfectly. I had only a few Colorado buff stones, and the shapes of those stones dictated the archway's ancient look. I loved building it because I was doing the exact same work stonemasons were doing hundreds of years ago.

ABOVE AND RIGHT: This large bathtub is surrounded in creamy Arizona buff flagstone. We polished it to match the elegant look of the bathroom.

23

TRADITIONAL STYLE

The homeowners of this traditional ranch property desired a traditional ashlar style of stonework for their home. Ashlar stones are those that have been shaped into rectangles, so ashlar stonework results in a very linear, orderly look.

In life, there are crossroads. When I decided to go out on my own and leave Cuyamungue Stone Company behind, it was a turning point in my life. I was thirty-three years old. It was far from a fear-free undertaking. There was the mortgage on my land and the prospect of keeping my family fed and clothed and cared for. I worried about getting through winters. Would jobs come? And where would they come from? A man once told me, "Buying land is the best thing you can ever do. You will come up with that payment every single month." And that's exactly what happened. While I was working with Robert Taylor, my stone style, characterized by tight joints and beautiful lines, developed a following. After I left, the jobs did come, most notably one of titanic scale on a ranch south of Santa Fe.

The ranch owners, the retired head of a major corporation and his wife, were remodeling their property. They decided to have stone floors installed, and my name came up. I was hired, I would get paid by the hour—and receive more per hour than I ever had before. Six months of not worrying where money was coming from. I was thrilled, young person that I was, that they would even consider me. But, young as I was, I was aware of all the other stonemasons in Santa Fe, and I had learned so much. I knew in the back of my mind that I could match them. Even though they were the "big guys" in town, a voice in me said, "I am going to be the best someday, and here is my opportunity to start proving it." That time was one of the happiest and hardest times in my life. Happiest because of the opportunity. Hardest because of the

challenge. As I began the floors, they gave me more to do: fireplaces, stone walls, and pillars.

First, we had to gather the stone. The ranch owners had yet another ranch, and we harvested the stone from that land. We were driven out to a remote part of New Mexico, deep into the heart of the terrain, on old, bumpy wagon paths. Finally, sheepherder huts came into view—rough-hewn structures of mud and stone, built in 1899 and 1904. We saw old barrels, tools, tin cans—evidence of lives lived out here, their workaday materials now relics. We pulled the sandstone from the huts, but only from structures that had collapsed. These stones would now have a new incarnation in tall, imposing fireplaces and chimneys.

Sandstone comes in many colors, from red to white to golden. It is so abundant in

the Southwest, and it comes in the colors of this region. That's what makes sandstone so unique to New Mexico and Santa Fe. People want to build with the colors of the earth, and there they are in stone. Even when you mix sandstone together, it all matches. I prefer the harder types of sandstone, as the softer versions can be so soft that they just crumble. They don't lend themselves to building or to the climate. The harder sandstones will stand up to being beaten with a hammer and a chisel and will weather the elements.

When the stones were in the sheepherder huts, they hadn't been worked—they were in rough, natural square and rectangular shapes. The shepherds found the flattest face of the stones and laid them like adobe bricks. When we took the stones and applied them to the fireplace at the ranch, we were guided by

the flattest face of the stone and went on to form them into more perfect rectangles.

Back at the ranch, the owner told me, "Go up six feet and then stop." I had my piles of rock. I was ready to show my stuff. I wanted so badly to do a great job and inspire confidence in my abilities, so I set the stones together tightly and perfectly. When I reached six feet, I stopped and summoned the owner.

The tension was high. The owner had the bearing of a president or a movie star—he looked like Cary Grant against the desert backdrop. His wife looked every inch a first lady. Their heads shook back and forth. "No." My heart sank. "Your stones are too close together."

I took it down and began again, this time setting the stones a little farther apart. The owner came back and stood before me in

Sandstone can achieve dark shades like this because of natural exposure to the elements.

his classic stance, his wife at his side. Once again, he shook his head. "No, I want the stones to be more rectangular, and I want the lines to be straighter." And again, my heart sank.

So I took it down once more, and by then, I was sure I knew exactly what he wanted. I kept my lines straight and shaped the stones into rectangles, which took a lot of work. He came back again. They both smiled and nodded. "That's it. That's the kind of stonework we have back at our ranch in Texas." I was pleased that they were happy, but I did wonder why they hadn't shown me a picture of what they wanted initially. Taking down that good solid work twice was a little soul-searing. But at least I was getting paid by the hour!

After that, I knew what he wanted and he knew I could do it. There were several trips back to the other ranch to get more stone. One of the challenges was that I was told to maintain the patina—the weathered look—on the faces of the stone. I wasn't able to work the faces of the stone extensively, because it would become a different color than the stone's natural patina. I could cut the top, back, bottom, and two sides, but very minimally the face.

Seventeen years later, the ranch owner passed away, and his wife decided that she wanted some more stonework done at the ranch. She called the contractor and said, "There was a young man who did that stonework for us, and I can remember that he had long blond hair and was a tall, skinny fellow." He said, "That's John Morris." After all of those years, she wanted me back to do the work. That felt good.

sandstone comes
in many colors, from red to white to golden. People want to build with the colors of the earth, and there they are in stone.

Though the pattern of this chimney looks very neat and arranged, it wasn't planned out. I build stone by stone, choosing the stone that will best fit the space that needs to be filled. The pattern naturally develops on its own.

I can see the owner nodding his head...
"Yes, that's what I want."

The stonework at this ranch is more on the traditional side of the spectrum, which wasn't what I'd gravitated toward thus far. However, the more stones I put together, the more I began to enjoy and like it. It added breadth to my experience. Knowing I could do it added to the confidence of a man just striking out on his own.

The amount of confidence I've gotten from each job I've finished is astounding, totally astounding. There are not a lot of jobs that baffle or overwhelm me like they did in the beginning. But I'm still learning from any project that I do, even the simplest one.

When I think back on the time I spent working at this ranch, I remember the wind most. The wind never rested there, and my ears were filled with its rushings and the flapping of a large American flag. There were days that the wind was in such a hurry that we were forced to go home. It wasn't safe to be up on the scaffolds. By the time we were done, the flag was so weathered and torn and frayed, the ranch owners had to get a new one. But in the face of those elements, I knew my stones would stand the test of time.

On the home's exterior, the varied color and texture of stone contrast nicely with plain expanses of stucco and red wooden gates.

I returned seventeen years later to add this work.

I love how this happy little gate looks between these two stone columns. The natural colors of the stone are a good backdrop for the barn red color.

ORGANIC BY DESIGN

ORGANIC BY DESIGN

This stone doorway was my interpretation of Indian ruins. The uneven pattern and differing sizes of stone create a more natural, less manufactured look.

The work I did on this house came about because of a conversation between a contractor, an architect, and a homeowner concerning a home in the shadow of the Santa Fe Opera. "We need to build a stone wall 350 feet long and nineteen feet tall at its highest point. Who can do it?" The contractor John Wolf said, "I think John Morris can do it." ◈ I wish that someone had snapped a picture of me back then, standing at the site of this future wall that I would, in fact, build—a wall that would run alongside a curving, twisting driveway up to a grand house on a hill. "Oh, my God," I thought. Can I really do this?" But I never let anyone know that I was questioning myself. "I can do this without a doubt," I told them. "I can pull this off."

We used New Mexico sandstone for this project because it's beautiful and hardy. The colors blend beautifully with the surrounding vistas, flora, and fauna. In the beginning of the November of a record-breaking snow season, I began. I picked up my first rock. "I'm not going to look behind and see how much work there is to be done here," I thought. I couldn't let myself get lost in the enormity of the project that lay ahead. I dealt with it one stone at a time.

I also realized that I was going to need help to build this wall—I couldn't do it alone. In hiring some men to help me and showing and teaching them how it was to be built, I trained some of the best workers and forged some of the best friendships of my life. Many still work with me, and they remain my friends.

Hour by hour, day by day, month by month, through rain, sleet, and snow, this wall began to take shape, and I finally got to the point where I realized, "I'm actually going to do this." And, "Wow, this is really beautiful."

Every morning we'd get in a huddle and psych ourselves up, just like in a football game. That energy lasted and built on itself all day long. We did not get bored. Every single rock in that wall had to be cut to fit. Every little rock now has its own story.

When the wall got to a certain height, we took our chisels and drove them in between the rocks, using them as a mountain climber would use pitons to stand on to reach that much higher. As the walls grew higher, we built scaffolds to be able to work from the platforms.

All of my work

is hand-chiseled, not done with saws and grinders. A more natural and better result can be had with the hammer and chisel.

There were a couple of rules that we followed when we built the wall. To ensure the wall's sturdiness, the face of any rock could not stand higher than its depth. We also crossed our vertical lines—we never had four corners in one spot. This is an ancient rule of stonemasonry, and we followed it like a commandment.

One day, it was snowing so hard that many of us couldn't make it up the hill to come to the job site. It was just me and my worker and friend Ben. We were on such a roll that day that we worked through the storm with five, six, eight inches of snow around us. We were infected by the thrill of the falling snow, like kids building a fort. Our hammers and chisels sang as we picked up stone after stone and found a home for each one in the mounting wall. I remember that day so

clearly—how we finally left at 3 p.m., and yet we couldn't wait to come back and resume our work.

All of my work is hand-chiseled, not done with saws and grinders. Many stonemasons are currently using saws and grinders. If you don't know how to work a hammer and chisel, it may seem easier to use saws and grinders than to learn how to do it the old-fashioned way. But in the long run, it's harder. The dirt, the dust, and the noise are ugly intrusions into one's day. A more natural result and better working environment can be had with the hammer and chisel.

The sound of the hammers hitting the chisels all day long is a chant, a prayer. It's better than any radio station you can dial into, and I mean that from my heart. I hear it from all different directions and distances—not the

The flowing curves of
the wall make it seem
timeless—organic and
one with its environment.

These stone doorways, made up of multicolored sandstones and large stone lintels, offer a kiva-like atmosphere for the dining area.

sound of diamond blades whining their way through rock, but the natural sound of the hammer and chisel in the stone.

My next challenge for this project was to make stone doorways for the house's round adobe dining room. The room was the architect's design, but I was given artistic free rein, with the directive to avoid a dated 1960s stacked-stone result. My inspiration was the organic look of Indian ruins.

We collected many shapes and colors of sandstone rocks. Following the principle of which stones fit best seemed to naturally include a balance of color and proportion. In order to ensure the preservation of the correct angles of walls, which were not plumb but on a slant, I attached strings from the ceiling to the floor and followed them as a guide.

We cut the large stones used as lintels to suit the round room's curve. To get them into place, we used scaffolding support and our combined strength to lift them and slide them into place. The lintels will be there for as long as they are allowed to be. Although the dining room table seats eight, the encircling shape of the room, the overlapping layered wooden ceiling, and the welcoming stacked-stone doorways give the room a feeling of warmth and intimacy rare in formal dining rooms.

In this house, all the floors are flagstone, the baseboards are stone, and the thresholds under the door are handmade from slabs of

in this house all the floors are flagstone, the baseboards are stone, and the thresholds under the door are handmade from slabs of stone.

Every detail in this home has a handcrafted yet organic look. The combination of the stone doorway and these beautiful handcarved wooden doors is stunning.

These multicolored, finely fitted sandstones add warmth, texture, and interest to the shepherd's bed fireplace.

STONE IN
THE FOREST

The gentle curve of this stone bench follows the curve of the property's landscaping.

Right around the corner from Canyon Road, Santa Fe's art gallery row, Monte Sol is an intimate grouping of high-end condos on the Chiaroscuro Gallery grounds. When we began the project for this complex of condos, we were told that we needed to build a small wall and a patio. But soon we were creating fireplaces, flagstone patios, and stacked-stone walls and stairs that would go in the forest-like courtyards. This project is a good representation of my hand-chiseled style of stonework and it shows how important it is to choose the right stone for the job. ✽ To achieve top-notch stonework, you have to have top-notch stone. I'm constantly approached by people with truckloads of stone, but way before the job begins, I'm extremely particular about the quality of the stone that will be used for the job. Stone might look very similar at first glance, but I've learned how to judge it.

The project was very architect-driven. The architect told me what he wanted for the property—steps here, wall there. But in executing it, I gave it my own style. It's one thing to draw a line on a piece of paper, but it's your wall once you build it: it no longer belongs to the piece of paper; it's no longer a concept; it's a reality with a signature.

I first had to choose the type of stone that would best fit the look and style of the property. When we started this project, the property had no landscaping, so I had to envision what the stone would look like outside when the landscaping was finished and had grown in. I knew the courtyard was eventually going to be a shady garden setting, so I needed to choose a material that would look at home among the trees and greenery. Native moss rock, a type of sandstone found in the forest that often has moss and lichens growing on it, was the perfect option.

We used full sheets of flagstone for Monte Sol's floors and patios, cut to fit together, instead of resorting to the use of smaller pieces. When working with smaller pieces, the look is more "jigsaw" than the elegant and abundant feeling of large pieces of flagstone. Large sheets make really nice tight joints, while small pieces give rise to more rustic-looking joints.

When I'm evaluating flagstone, not only do I look at the surface of the stone (which may well be perfectly smooth), I look at the edge of the stone. I can tell whether that stone is going to fall apart, whether it will crumble when I start chiseling. When I hit it, I listen to hear if it has a ring to it. If it makes a dead "dung" sound, it's layered too much and it's going to spall (flake).

We used full sheets of flagstone for Monte Sol's floors and patios, cut to fit together, instead of resorting to the use of smaller pieces.

Over and over again, I hear homeowners and landscape architects complain about how sandstone flakes. Nine times out of ten, sandstone flakes because it's not installed with an eye toward proper drainage. A good outdoor stone floor needs to be installed at a quarter-inch per foot angle. The surface still registers to the eye as level, even with that slight incline. Drainage is more critical with stone floors than beauty or fit. Even the hardest concrete will deteriorate if water collects on its surface and sits there.

If stone is allowed to shed moisture, it will last indefinitely. Some stones simply do not work for patios or floors, but it's the job of the stonemason to know the quality and appropriateness of stone. Many times, architects will draw up plans for the exterior patios of a home designed around an eighth-inch per foot—but many stones are bowed an eighth-inch within themselves. Even though the stone appears to be level, it's not. There's a pitch to it.

The ring, the sound, the shape—all are criteria for the fitness of a stone to a project. When working with walls, we don't choose pie-wedge-shaped stones or round stones (what we call cow-pie stones). We look for stones with crisp square edges. We look for quality and hardness. There are certain sandstones that are too soft to work with. When we begin to fine-tune this type of stone, it crumbles. On the other hand, sandstone that's too hard is often fractured. Fractured stone has cracks in it, and when it is hit, it can fall apart at the fracture lines. I want a solid stone. If I have to take that stone and heat on it for an hour or more, I want to still have that stone in front of me at the end and not a pile of gravel.

In the moment of creation, I'm not watch-

For this project, we used native moss rock, a type of sandstone found in the woods.

ing the clock or concerning myself with how long I have until I go home. I'm concerned with the rock I'm fitting in that wall. I could spend two hours with one rock and ten minutes with the next one. Each one is so totally different. Rarely does a rock just fit in a wall. I always have to do something with it. Even if it does fit, I may have to go back and chip the top so the next one doesn't give me a lot of trouble.

I fit the stones together, but I still allow them to be natural as opposed to forcing them to be rectangles or squares. I'm trying to maintain the stones—the shapes—the way they are. For instance, when I made the steps to the courtyards, I found stones that could serve as both riser and tread—one thick rectangle—not different stones pieced together.

The colors of New Mexican stones just automatically fit in perfectly with the land. Even though these stones vary in color, they're all from New Mexico and they blend in beautifully here. When I complete a wall, the colors of the stone look a certain way, but they will change. Six months or a year later, weather and lime change the colors of the stone. It's like you are looking in a kaleidoscope, where the colors shift with one fraction of a turn. But that fraction of a turn is six or eight months.

It's gratifying to visit this site and see all of our work settled into its location, surrounded by plants and flowers, as if it were always there.

Moss rock comes from the forest. Its dark surface, sometimes covered with green, and rugged texture look right at home in a wooded setting such as this.

The stairs are made out of
single natural stones.

A cool bench in the shade is a welcome place to rest. This beautiful seating area is made of native New Mexico moss rock and buff flagstone.

OLD-WORLD HACIENDA

Polished flagstone floors contribute to the elegant, high-end look of this foyer.

I think I knew for sure that I had "made it" when I was called for the Rancho Alegre job. Rancho Alegre is an estate modeled after a New Mexican town of old with its own chapel, a bunkhouse (to serve as guest accommodations), a watchtower (*torreon*), and, of course, the grand hacienda—an entire little scene that would remind you of a Wild West town even though it was a residence. The owner, Mike Kammerer, and the contractor, John Wolf, wanted the finest stonework available—and they called me to discuss this very large undertaking. In addition to the elements mentioned above, we'd also need to install flagstone floors throughout the main residence, a porphyry driveway, a pool with an infinity edge, and a master bedroom and bathroom (well, more of a bath suite) of stacked stone, modeled after Chaco Canyon's ruins.

A partial view of the Rancho Alegre "village," with its chapel and protecting torreon.

We began with the torreon. Mike and John wanted it to be constructed of natural New Mexican sandstone in all of that stone's colors: gold, russet, brown, orange, white, black, gray, shades of red, and even tan rocks laced through with blue. I was in total agreement. When you see the rocks all piled on the truck, they almost look like they're the same color. But once you put them into a project, the rain and the snow and the climate bring out the tones of each rock more and more as the years pass. If you had a white rock, you'd think that it would become whiter with the sun and the rain—but it doesn't. It becomes darker.

Unlike a classic stone wall, we didn't try to mold the stones into square blocks. We used as much of the stone as we could, which resulted in beautiful wild designs, almost like a glass mosaic. The natural shapes of the stones dictated the story of the tower's growth—we didn't mold the stones into anything besides their organic shapes. Just like a tailor chooses to work with the natural flow of a cloth, we did the same with the stones. It felt like we wove the stones together . . . and we ended up with a beautiful flowing wall. Six stonemasons helped me build this stone tower, and we had piles and piles of stones to choose from when looking to fit them into the spaces that needed to be filled.

The torreon wall grew to the point where we needed scaffolding. We tied all the scaffolds together in a circle around the tower, and I set up a pulley that would bring stone up to the top. Once we were twenty-five feet up in the air, with rocks piled on all sides and chisels singing, we were safe from the rattlesnakes below, and most of the spiders, and it was a great feeling. We were up there having fun, and we could even turn the radio

on because we didn't need to keep our ears open for the sound of a rattle.

Because of the energy and flow that my helpers and I had going, we built that whole thing in a month and a half . . . pretty darn fast. We were lucky. We had a really good supply of rock and good weather, and we were in a groove.

I've done big projects on my own, and there's a peace of mind to that, always working your own spot, always being that one man: one man working his stone alone is magical. There's rhythm, a pace, a whole thing set up that you step right into. That energy, speed, space, and flow carry on day in and day out.

But six or seven men working together don't do seven times as much as that one man can do. They're doing three times seven times that, just by the way that the group's energy amasses. It's exponential. But all it takes is one person to be out of sync to throw the whole dance off. One bad player can ruin the whole game. My team is tight—we've all become really good friends and can anticipate each other's moves.

Historically, torreons served as watch-towers. This torreon could actually be used for that purpose should the need arise. To get to the top, you climb a sturdy wooden ladder. This ladder was made by the Indians at the Santo Domingo pueblo, and it is so big and heavy that it had to be craned into place. You can stand up there and look out in any direction you choose. Mr. Kammerer was trying to re-create the feeling of a little western village or town. Old torreons that truly did serve as watchtowers once are all over the place in this state.

ABOVE AND RIGHT:
European-style porphyry
paving, combined with
handcrafted doors and
Colonial-style lanterns,
creates an old-world
look and feel.

Once we finished the torreon, we moved on to the chapel, where we began to install Colorado red flagstone floors. We were instructed to give the floor an older feeling by using looser, more rustic joints—more space between the stones—which is unlike my usual style. You often find the "old stone look" in New Mexico churches. It was done by people in the parish community who weren't necessarily stonemasons, who put down stones to have a floor, period, not to display skilled artisanship. They were volunteers working together. Mr. Kammerer wanted that sense of authenticity.

Twice in my life, I've been able to make as much noise as I wanted to in a church. The first time was when I lowered the altar of the church at the San Ildefonso Pueblo. That altar was made of Vermont slate brought in on the railroad many years before. The priests wanted to communicate that they were on the same level as the people, so they asked us to remove the platform and put the altar back on the ground. In that church, and in Rancho Alegre's chapel, sound was amplified to that of a rock-and-roll concert.

FLOORS

My flagstone floors always seem to get me in the door when it comes to getting jobs. Inevitably, people who are building a house end up seeing one of my stone floors somewhere else, and the first words out of their mouths are, "Who did that floor?" My floors have a look that can only come from hand-chiseled stonework. There are guys cutting stone with saws and grinders and doing a good job, but they are never able to capture the beauty of a hand-chiseled floor. It can't be done. They'll cut with a grinder and then chip the edges to make it look

RIGHT: This fan pattern
is typical of old street
paving in Europe.

FACING: This fireplace
is graced by hand-
chipped, honed, and
polished flagstone
seating and floors.

more natural. But the only way to do it right
is to take a hammer and chisel and throw
the saws and grinders away. A floor that has
been shaped with a saw and grinder has a
machined look to it. With even the smallest
grinder, you can't make those erratic lines
that you can make with a half-inch chisel or
give it that broken look. Even if you cut with
a grinder and then come back and nip at it
with a chisel, you still have that machined
line that you can't interrupt. And the stones
start to look completely unnatural. My floors
look like hand-tooled leather pieces that are
massaged together to flow and harmonize.
You can feel the handiwork because it's
closest to the organic nature of stone.

I also developed my own way of creating
these floors. By raising the stone I'm shaping an inch or so above the space I'm trying
to fill and then chipping away until the stones
beneath are revealed, I make the perfect

joint without having to use templates. That
line becomes a perfect match for the stones
underneath it. All of those beautiful edges are
captured with just a hammer and chisel. I'm a
nibbler when it comes to stonework—nibble at
the stone. I'm not trying to cut the whole front
edge of the stone at one time, but instead I
peck away at it like a woodpecker to take away
just the stone that I want to remove.

I always try to avoid pointed triangles,
whether it's a floor or a wall. I follow this

little rule: when you cut a stone and set it, you have to remember the one that's going to come afterward. If it's impossible to cut it to fit without breaking it, you're not in good shape. You have to think about the one that comes next and remember to accommodate it.

The floors I've made contain the story of my life. I've spent so many years of my life on my knees, making floors. Now that I'm getting into the second half of my life, I need to stretch my legs more. I can't kneel as much as I used to. But I miss it.

It got to where I could kneel on a stone and lift the hammer and chisel to cut that stone, and I could hear the stone telling me things: "Don't hit it right there because it might break" or "Hit it over here so it won't break." I can tell by the ring of the stone whether it's a solid stone or whether it wants to shatter. I've heard sculptors say the same

thing. You can feel the sound of the stone in your knees when you cut it, giving you direction on how to cut it right. When you do it day in and day out, you're able to feel sound with your body, just like blind persons learn to orient themselves without the sense of sight.

PORPHYRY DRIVEWAY

Porphyry is one of the most durable paving stones available on the planet. Used all over the world, it's harder than granite. But I had never worked with it before encountering it on this assignment. It's not indigenous to New Mexico or the Southwest. We imported this porphyry from Mexico. I didn't have any trouble setting it in the courtyard or around the chapel or by the bunkhouse. But when it came to the repeating fan patterns desired for the driveway, I knew that I needed to learn how to do that from an expert.

Porphyry looks like the stone in so many of the streets in Europe. It's a very hard red, green, or purple igneous rock. "Porphyry" comes from the Greek word for purple. It has been used for roads for centuries because it's very hard and durable. I found myself thinking of the miles and miles of porphyry that were installed before I was born. As large of an area as I worked on, my job was miniscule, a drop in the bucket in the miles of porphyry that are all over Spain and Italy. It's probably as close to being an eternal stone as any. As hard as it is, when you start looking at these ancient applications, you can see where it's been polished and smoothed by the traffic of man. While I'm working with porphyry, I think about how long it actually takes to walk a path to create that worn look: how many cars, bicycles, wooden wagon wheels "finished" these roads?

Mr. Kammerer brought Hector Furione

to me from Mexico. Originally from Italy, he worked with the Mexican quarry that sent us the porphyry stone. A few hours each day for a week, he showed me his tricks of the trade: how to lay out the stone, how to get it level, how to make it repeat itself evenly. Sometimes he showed me that I just had to use my eye to gauge it. All of this learning took place in either Spanish or Italian.

When we got started, we had thousands of square feet in front of us to do. And then we got into the curved parts of the driveway. Everything Hector had taught me was off of a square plane, and now I had to adjust it to work off curves. It was quite challenging. Working with the fan patterns really came down to mathematics. You're always working with that radius, be it fifty-four inches or another measurement. You begin with a point in space and then decide how far a line will

RIGHT AND FACING:
Sierra stone serves as
a handsome backdrop
for these jewelry display
cases. Each piece has a
landscape of its own.

extend from the point in a fan arc. It's an easily repeating pattern, because each end of the arc is the point where another arc begins.

Mr. Kammerer was really pressuring us to finish the driveway because it was the very last thing to do on the house. It must have been 110 degrees outside. Working on that driveway in that heat with that stone was so onerous that we all came close to passing out. We pulled it off, though; we finished the job.

JEWELRY CASES

I always like the opportunity to work with unusual materials. Porphyry was one. When we worked on the main residence's master bathroom and the jewelry cases set into the walls that led to it, we worked with Sierra stone.

Sierra stone is rather hard to come by and it's expensive. It comes from Utah and Arizona and has a beautiful embossed-looking texture, characterized by wavy lines. It's a striking backdrop for the rare Indian jewelry that rests against it, making the most unusual jewelry cases I've ever seen. The jewelry cases are set into the wall the way a nicho would be so that the jewelry could be both stored and on display at all times, not just seen when it was worn. It has the feeling of a museum display setup, while the stone adds an element of warmth that allows the cases to blend in well in a domestic setting. We also

The bands

of stone are actually two inches high (in between little stacked stones). Little ones are one-sixteenth inch, one-eighth inch, and up to one-half inch.

used it as a backsplash for the bathroom sink. In this case, we sandblasted the Sierra stone to pull up more three-dimensional relief. When you sandblast this stone, the lighter parts are eaten away more easily because they're softer than the darker areas. We cut the backsplash stone into a silhouette that evoked a mountain range vista.

The use of Sierra stone is a perfect example of all the little details that make Rancho Alegre so special. There were no corners cut; Kammerer never took the cheap way out. Anywhere we worked in that house, we did our best to capture the full spirit of the stone and bring it out, even if we were working behind a door. It was the energy of the project.

Nowhere is that exemplified more than in the bathroom, where the walls are fully made of thin stacked stone. Let me restate that. The very high, very large walls are made of pains-

takingly collected and stacked thin stone.

Mike Kammerer actually drove to Chaco Canyon and took pictures of a certain stacked stone wall there, with a tape measure propped against it. Chaco Canyon is within Chaco Culture National Historical Park in New Mexico, a preserve of stone-quarried pueblos built by ancient indigenous people of the region. Anasazi stacked stone is inspired by the stonework found at Chaco Canyon.

After he showed me that picture and told me what he wanted, I put up a small sample on the wall of his bedroom, using little tiny pieces of stone. When he granted his approval, I realized that my journey had just begun. Where in the world would I find all of these skinny little rocks to re-create the look of Anasazi ruins?

The bands of stone are actually two inches high (in between little stacked stones). Little ones are one-sixteenth inch, one-eighth inch,

and up to one-half inch. I needed a lot—not just a bucket- or a wheelbarrow- or a pallet-full. I needed truckloads and truckloads of stone. Any time I saw thin, thin pieces of stone, I would pick them up, even it was just one. I'd split them down when the stone would allow it. I'd search stoneyards. I combined everything that I'd ever saved or collected with everything I found new.

This is the biggest bathroom I've ever been in, with the largest, most impressive showers I've ever seen. The floors are heated, so the space is a lot warmer than it looks. While you are taking a shower, you can look to your left and see the water coming over the top of the wall, running down twelve feet of wall into a pool, with a gorgeous statue sitting in that pool. Next to that is a bathtub. There's a beautiful little fireplace in the corner to add to the experience. The door passageways going in and out of the bathroom are done in the tradi-

tional shape or form of Anasazi doorways. We also installed vigas on which to hang the towels. Along the top of the walls in the bathroom are the stone lights with an angled stone tilting to create just the right amount of subtle light.

When you walk into this space, instead of having a first impression of a cold, heavy stone bathroom, you're lifted into a warm, sacred space, an inviting space. By no means do you feel closed in; you feel enlightened. You know you're someplace really special, seeing something that not just anybody gets to see. I feel so lucky that Mike let the world see that in this book.

The stacked stone, the small illuminated "windows," the presence of a ladder, the open floorplan—everything contributes to the feeling that you're in a subterranean Anasazi dwelling.

FACING: The pool and waterfall were created to showcase this Michael Naranjo sculpture.

ABOVE: This partition wall of stacked stone adds privacy in the master bedroom.

RIGHT: Handcarved stone is a wonderful element used as a spout to fill the tub.

The shapes
of these
passageways
were inspired by
Chaco Canyon's
ancient wall
openings.

Being in this room is a spiritual experience. All of the details capture the solemn atmosphere of an Anasazi kiva.

The natural
pattern of the Sierra
stone creates the look of
a mountain range
that serves
as a backsplash for
the master
bathroom's sink.

FACING: This indoor torreon creates an unusual circular bathroom.

ABOVE AND ABOVE RIGHT: The back of the nicho is made of slate, which was found with this naturally occurring pattern that looks like a handmade motif. It's surrounded by blocks of Hackett stone, which comes from Arkansas.

LOWER RIGHT: Hackett stone has varied colors and an interesting rough texture. It is one of the densest stones I've ever worked with.

This shepherd's fireplace is made of Hackett stone. Notice how the one large stone above the hearth makes up the shepherd's bed.

The risers and treads of the steps
are made of solid individual stones.

Sometimes you don't know how a fireplace will
turn out until you gather the rocks, and the rocks yell at you,
telling you which way they should go.

A sculpture entitled *The Healer* by artist Joe Beeler overlooks an infinity edge pool. Flagstone paving surrounds the pool.

A ROMAN BATH

Using travertine helped create an authentic Roman look, since travertine was one of the most common building materials in ancient Rome.

This bathroom is a perfect example of how beautiful and dramatic stonework can be in a small space. You notice the details, not the dimensions. The homeowner, Mr. DeMay, wanted the room to be lined in stone blocks to evoke the feeling of à Roman bathroom. However, the room was so small that we realized that if we put actual blocks there, the room would feel too cramped. We had the challenge of making one-inch-deep New Mexico travertine stone tiles look like blocks. I realized that if I chipped the edges, they registered to the eye as blocks when set into the wall. I had a vision of the Roman look that Mr. DeMay wanted, and I had to create it with the travertine stone that he picked.

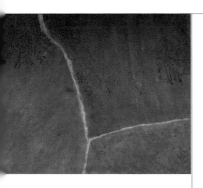

ABOVE: Outside the bathroom, finely fitted flagstones feature beautiful natural dendrites in the stone. Dendrites are treelike patterns formed by mineral deposits in rock.

FACING: A built-in heated stone bench was placed in the shower.

The lintel above the shower entrance is cracked—intentionally. The client felt that everything looked too new, and he wanted to give the room a sense of age by making the lintel look like it had fractured over time, perhaps in an earthquake. Other challenges followed: making the towel and toilet paper holders out of stone; hiding drawers in the walls without knobs so that they look like stone blocks until you pull them out by slipping your finger into an indentation.

I made the natural stone sink myself. I love making stone bowls—they're a lot of fun. If you were to pick a material to make a bowl from, the most difficult one would be stone. People look at a stone bowl, and they're bewildered at the thought of how it was made. But once you begin removing stone from the center of a rock, it amazes me how easy it is. As an exception to my usual rule, in the case of making a stone bowl, I use power tools to make the initial cuts. A beautiful stone bowl is usable art. The client had already bought a stone sink from another source, but that sink was made in China and didn't match the local stone. We would have to make one for him. When I told him how much it would cost, an alarmed look arose in his eyes. "This stone sink from China only cost x amount. Why is yours so much more?" My answer to him was: "We make more than a dollar a day here in Santa Fe, unlike they do in China."

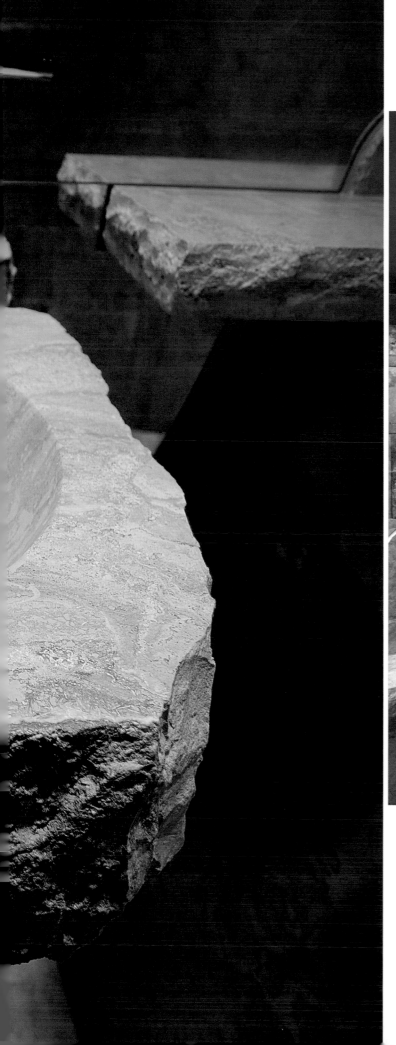

FACING: I sought out a huge solid piece of travertine to carve the sink from so that it would exactly match the rest of the stone in the bathroom.

ABOVE: Stone towel hooks were made especially for this project.

ABOVE AND FACING: Stone-veneered drawers are only recognizable as drawers when open.

LEFT: We purposely broke this lintel to make it look old.

LEFT: All the tiles have hand-chipped edges to give the feeling that the walls are made of blocks.

FACING: You won't find this at Home Depot.

LIMESTONE
BEAUTY

Though you might think of limestone as white, it can actually exhibit many colors, like the ones in this limestone wall.

Limestone is a classic building stone. Many medieval churches and castles in Europe were built with limestone because of its durability and accessibility. I love working with this stone in the landlocked desert of New Mexico. Sometimes I come upon a fossilized imprint of a seashell or sea creature. To be suddenly reminded that this part of the continent was once covered by ocean is a powerful thing. You could write a whole book just on limestone. Limestone out of Indiana is considered some of the finest in the world; it's used to make statues, gargoyles, and cornices. It's the perfect stone for carving; it's almost fractureless. On the other end of the spectrum, there is the hard, hard limestone from New Mexico that's almost like glass.

ABOVE: The new entry sign for the Bishop's Lodge is hand-chiseled for a natural-looking edge.

FACING: One rugged stone wall can add so much visual impact to a building.

that stands out is that we built a perfect true arch over the firebox, which was challenging.

Several years later, the Bishop's Lodge folks came back to me, requesting that I build their stone signs. I used the same stone for the wall encircling the sign, which is made out of sandstone, not limestone. When we took down the older sign, we noticed that it was very poorly built. It was dated 1970. Back then, the awareness of good stonemasonry just wasn't very high. On the other hand, it had been there so long that I felt like I was taking down a part of history. My goal in replacing the wall and the sign was to try to create something that looked like it was always there, instead of a brand new glittering sign—something that melded into its environment, an instant part of the community.

The use of large stones in uneven, natural shapes creates a rustic look perfect for a lodge. Notice the variation in color from light to dark.

STONE IN THE MODERN IDIOM

STONE IN THE MODERN IDIOM

Leaving the surface of the stone rough and natural results in more texture and variety in color.

When we took on this residence, a home with a very linear geometric design, we knew that the rough, natural stones would have to be subdued into corresponding neat, geometrically regular blocks. The exterior of this home is unique, as it consists entirely of steel, glass, and stone. It doesn't contain any stucco or painted siding, which is not something we come across too often. Additionally, instead of flowing with what the stones want to do, as in the case of the Rancho Alegre torreon, every stone in the residence was battered and coerced into shape before being fitted into this home. We weren't working with the natural shapes of the stone; we were meeting dimensions. Not one stone could be over eight inches tall. The walls were of varying heights. This made the design very linear, very horizontal. It's a beautiful house.

the sound

of hammer on the chisel . . . like the chirping of birds in trees, the sound of your own breathing. Once it stops, the silence comes in, and that's loud.

FACING: Every rock doesn't end up in a wall.

Every day, my good friend Roger Rivera pulled up in his one-ton super-duty truck with a load of New Mexico sandstone (or "moss rock"). It's called moss rock because moss often grows on it, giving it more interest, texture, and color. When Roger showed up, my guys and I swarmed his truck like fish in a fish tank swimming toward the sprinkles of fish food. We swarmed, massed, converged— anxious for these new blocks of stone, this new batch of fresh shapes for us. It was like we were kids and the ice cream man had pulled up. We had choice piles of rock to cut and shape, but then at the end of the day we were down to leftovers once again. Productivity slowed down as the hours passed, and we had to pick through the leftovers because all the good stones were now in the walls. We looked forward to the next day when the truck of new stone appeared. It was a little cycle that happened every single day.

The sound of the hammer on the chisel is a sound of that job site that we became so accustomed to. It's like the chirping of birds in trees, the sound of your own breathing. Once it stops, the silence comes in, and that's loud. It's louder, somehow, than the rhythmic din. It has finality, but the stopping is always a pause, like the silence between ocean waves, the still moment between an inhale and exhale of breath. Thank God it never ends.

To me, there's a reward to seeing my work years later with the landscaping in place. It's no longer a construction site—the combination makes it all ring true.

The openings in the wall
and the main corridor of
the house were designed
to line up with true north
and south.

BENCHES, TABLES, AND STANDING STONES

This duo looks married, or like a brother and sister, but they were actually completely different stones that I was able to envision together to create this relationship.

By the swimming pool, under a pinon tree, in a field of flowers . . . just a rock at the shoreline is a bench for watching the sea. The most popular benches we make are the ones closest to nature; the most natural-looking ones are slabs of stone put together. Sometimes I can find three rocks and have a stone bench. Sometimes I find one rock and have a stone bench. ✇ My work with standing stones is the most poetic thing I do because it's not about function, it's about beauty. Standing stones are stones that are acknowledged as art for what they are, without having to serve a pragmatic function. People purchase standing stones for the same reason they buy a painting, a piece of jewelry, or a piece of pottery.

Finding the natural slabs of stone to create the table is as much of a challenge as making it. But each unique piece of stone means a completely unique table.

The imperfections
of the stone
revealed through color,
texture, and crevices
become the
painted canvas that
only nature can
truly create.

ABOVE: I made this arch on the spur of the moment—I stacked the stones as a little challenge to myself at my stoneyard. No tools, no mortar . . . just nature.

FACING: The right side of the arch rests on an outcropping of a massive vertical stone.

you achieve the feeling that you've put something into the universe that's holy. It's the bliss of facilitating fittingness. I feel that all of my previous knowledge of working with stones throughout the years brought me to the place where I can achieve that harmony, envision it, execute it, and appreciate it. Perhaps I took this stone from its original home, but by putting it together so well with a mate, by carrying through with my vision of where this stone could be most beautiful, I can give this stone another life, another eternity.

Someone can get lucky standing these stones, but to really stand them up and to get them to belong takes more than luck. Touching and shaping stones your whole life—building, moving, stacking trucks, unstacking trucks, moving stones in a wheelbarrow—give you the knowledge of how to stand the stones and find their homes. You

have a relationship. You're able to deal with these rocks almost on their own level, the level of eternity.

I think of lumberjacks cutting down trees, of forests being cleared for use as products, and when I see the amount of stone that is in the world, I can't help but think that God intended us to build with stone. Stone doesn't burn and doesn't need to be painted or maintained. But as time goes on, we use stone less and less while cutting down more of the forest and using other materials that are so temporary and have such a finite timeline. Stone will never wear out, and it's so abundant. God gave us these rocks to use, to build with, to look at, and to love.

In creating something like this, it's not a simple matter of standing the stones and laying one across the top, but of carefully fitting them so that they are balanced perfectly or as close to perfect as I can get them.

LEFT: These three stones weren't found together, but they look like they are part of a family.

FACING: These two make me think of twins sharing the same heart.

LEFT AND RIGHT: These groupings of stones mark the beginning and end of a home's long drive. In the example on the right, architect Adrian DeWitt told me that he wanted to create an entrance that was different than the traditional pillared stone entrance or gated entryway. Within a week, I had found the stones that would lend themselves perfectly to the project. They went together with ease, like a perfect song being sung.